Grandma Owl is the
smartest bird that lives
in the forest.

She knows about the weather.

She knows what to do
in a storm.

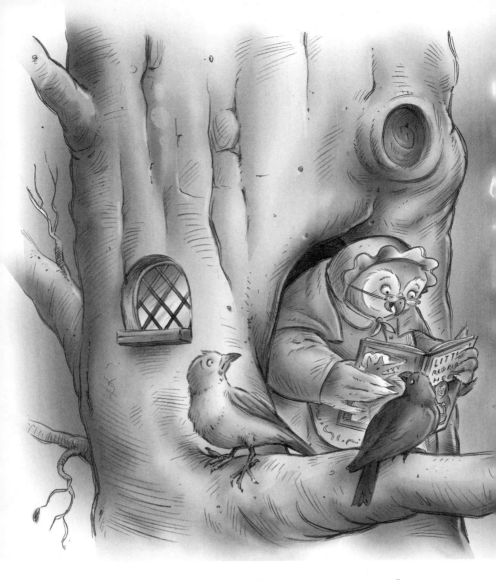

When thunder scares the
other birds, Grandma Owl
reads to them.

4

One book that she reads
is a fairy tale about a little
girl in a red bonnet.

Another book is about a
gingerbread boy.

Grandma Owl reads until
the storm is over.

The next day, the birds fly
over to thank Grandma Owl,
but she is fast asleep!